SIMPLY JESUS

LifeChange Books

JOE STOWELL

Multnomah®Publishers *Sisters, Oregon*

SIMPLY JESUS
published by Multnomah Publishers, Inc.

© 2002 by Dr. Joseph M. Stowell
International Standard Book Number: 1-57673-856-6

Cover design by David Carlson
Cover image by SuperStock

Unless otherwise indicated, Scripture quotations are from:
New American Standard Bible® © 1960, 1977, 1995
by the Lockman Foundation. Used by permission.
Other Scripture versions used:
The Holy Bible, New International Version (NIV) © 1973, 1984 by International Bible
Society, used by permission of Zondervan Publishing House
The Holy Bible, King James Version (KJV)
The Holy Bible, New Living Translation (NLT) © 1996. Used by permission of
Tyndale House Publishers, Inc. All rights reserved.
The Message © 1993 by Eugene H. Peterson

Multnomah is a trademark of Multnomah Publishers, Inc.,
and is registered in the U.S. Patent and Trademark Office.
The colophon is a trademark of Multnomah Publishers, Inc.

Printed in the United States of America

For information:
MULTNOMAH PUBLISHERS, INC. • P.O. BOX 1720 • SISTERS, OR 97759

Library of Congress Cataloging-in-Publication Data

Stowell, Joseph M.
  Simply Jesus / by Joesph M. Stowell.
    p. cm.
  ISBN 1-57673-856-6
  1. Christian life.   2. Jesus Christ—Person and offices.   I. Title.
  BV4509.5 .S85 2002
  248.4—dc21
                                                          2001006382

06 07 08—10 9 8 7 6 5

Table of Contents

Chapter 1

EXPERIENCING JESUS

*Paul said that it was the throbbing ambition
of his life to experience Jesus.... Is it yours?*

When my secretary told me I'd been invited to the White
House, my heart picked up a little speed.

I wonder if I'll get to meet the president.

Like everyone else, I'd read a lot about him and seen him
countless times in pictures and on TV. I'd followed his political career with more than a little interest. In fact, I had
voted for him. If someone had asked if I knew much about
him, I could have launched into a rather extensive description
of his background, his political philosophy, and his policies.

But this was different.

I was on the verge of actually experiencing him.
Personally.

Wearing my best navy pin-striped suit, a starched

white shirt, and a "presidential" tie, I stopped long enough at the airport to get my shoes professionally shined. I could hardly keep myself from telling the man bent over my feet, *Do a good job—these shoes are headed for the White House.*

I felt sobered as I walked into the grand foyer of our president's home. *These truly are the halls of power,* I said to myself. *Behind closed doors in this very house wars have been declared—history made.*

I found myself seated on the front row of the East Room. The small gathering hushed as a commanding voice announced, "Ladies and gentlemen, the president of the United States." We stood as he walked in briskly and took his place on the low platform. I couldn't take my eyes off of him. I was in his presence and found myself intrigued by his every move. Later, in a very brief conversation, I was surprised at how engaged he seemed. If only for a moment, he looked into my eyes and gave me his attention.

Frankly, having experienced the reality of his presence, I will never view our president in the same way again. I went away wishing I could know him better.

It's like that in your relationship with Jesus: You can be satisfied to just know about Him, or you can enter into an experience with Jesus. Only you can make the choice. And this choice determines the difference between religion as usual or the satisfaction of connecting with Jesus, the One we were created to enjoy.

More than Mere Knowledge

We all know who Jesus is. Right?

In the last two thousand years, no other individual has commanded such respect, such honor. Our entire Western civilization—from its laws to its ethics—has been marked and molded by His teaching. For over two millennia, history's greatest works of art have centered on His life, death, and resurrection. Enduring musical masterpieces have celebrated His worth and glory. But for those who have personally embraced the liberating reality of His forgiveness of sin and hope of eternity, He is so much more.

Or…at least, He should be.

We preach and teach about His will and His ways; tell His stories by heart; celebrate Him in worship; and serve Him with enthusiasm. Yet underneath it all (if we are truly candid), there is a gnawing sense that there should be something…well, more to this relationship.

Why is it that He often feels so far away? So historical? So church related? So other? The distance between knowing Him and knowing about Him is vast. And the space between these two experiences separates the spectators from intimate participants.

Think carefully. It's a pretty safe bet that if you are reading this book you know at least something about Him. You know something about Him biographically and historically.

In your more lucid moments, you might even be able to talk a little theology. But as impressive as your knowledge about Jesus may be, the unfortunate reality is that most of us stop there. Seemingly satisfied that knowing about Him is enough, we have no clue that there is more.

And there is more.

The thought of a deep richness waiting for those who get beyond knowing about Him to actually experiencing Him has either escaped us or—worse yet—has been exiled to the vague regions of religious wishful thinking.

If that's your story, get ready.

The best is yet to come.

Jesus intends for you to experience the pleasure and reassuring peace of His presence at the core of your life. He wants to be more than just another volume in your ency-clopedia of biblical facts. He didn't die for you to simply strike a deal guaranteeing heaven. He died for you to make you His own and to grant you the unspeakable privilege of experiencing Him personally.

As Paul wrote to early followers of Jesus...

He [God] is the one who invited you into this wonderful friendship with his Son, Jesus Christ.

1 CORINTHIANS 1:9, NLT

And think of this invitation that Jesus extends to all of us who will respond...

"Look! Here I stand at the door and knock. If you
hear me calling and open the door, I will come in,
and we will share a meal as friends."

Revelation 3:20, nlt

This is incomparably better than an invitation to the
White House. The eternal God of the universe has called us
into fellowship—friendship, companionship, close contact—with His Son. Jesus never intended to connect only
with your head; He lives to connect with the entire you. In
fact, He sent us the Holy Spirit to make the total connection possible, and gave us His Word to show the way. And,
regardless of who you are or how you have chosen to live
your life, you can know the pleasure of His presence.

Up close and personal.

Forgive a trip down memory lane, but I long again to
experience Jesus in my grandmother's quavery voice as she
sang the words of her favorite hymn:

I come to the garden alone
While the dew is still on the roses,
And the voice I hear falling on my ear
The Son of God discloses.
And He walks with me and He talks with me
and He tells me I am His own.
And the joy we share as we tarry there,
None other has ever known.

Knowing my grandmother, I have little doubt that she had moved well beyond simply "knowing about Him" into the joy of experiencing Him.

And just in case you think that a closer relationship with Jesus is about some kind of rigid morning routine, some tedious-but-essential religious exercise, think again. While regular Bible study and cultivating a life of prayer are indispensable, there is far more to a personal experience with Jesus.

—*It's about a deep and abiding sense of His nearness on the journey.*

—*It's about an unshakable confidence that only His abiding presence can give.*

—*It's about courage in the face of previously intimidating encounters.*

—*It's about a closeness that enables your spirit to commune with Him, anywhere, anytime, regardless.*

—*It's about meeting Him in places you may have never dreamed of…in the most heated of seductions, in the midst of suffering, and in acts of unflinching surrender.*

There is a marvelously mystical aspect to all this. You can't wrap words around it. You can't put it in a box and tie it up with a red ribbon. When you try to fully define it, you degrade it.

Jesus is never predictable. Just totally available. He

doesn't play hide-and-seek. In fact, He consistently rewards anyone who diligently seeks Him (Hebrews 11:6). But to many of us, tasting of that reward seems so illusive. Could it be we simply don't know how to seek Him or where to find Him?

I'll never forget the frustrating experience early one Sunday morning when I was supposed to pick up an elderly relative who had come into Chicago on the train from Milwaukee. The whole purpose of the exercise was to find her and get her safely to our house. I showed up on time, but where was she? Certainly not where I thought she would be. I checked the monitor and the train was already in. With a sinking feeling in the pit of my stomach, I scoured the early morning loneliness of Union Station...to no avail.

I was about ready to leave when I happened to glance down a hallway toward the baggage area. There she was, luggage at her feet, patiently waiting for me to arrive. She'd been there all the time. And to my chagrin, she was right where she should have been! I had been looking in all the wrong places.

The great news is that Jesus is there, patiently waiting for you. In fact, He not only waits, but is also at this very moment busily pursuing you. The fact that you are reading this book is no accident, no coincidence. It's just another one of the countless ways He hopes to get your attention.

It's time to connect.

YOU CAN'T GET ENOUGH OF HIM

The following lines of Scripture have captured my heart in recent days. Don't skip over them. Don't let your mind wander. If you really want to experience Jesus, you must read these words slowly and thoughtfully...until they have gripped your heart.

> I once thought all these things were so very important, but now I consider them worthless because of what Christ has done. Yes, everything else is worthless when compared with the priceless gain of knowing Christ Jesus my Lord. I have discarded everything else, counting it all as garbage, so that I may have Christ and become one with him. I no longer count on my own goodness or my ability to obey God's law, but I trust Christ to save me. For God's way of making us right with himself depends on faith. *As a result, I can really know Christ and experience the mighty power that raised him from the dead.* I can learn what it means to suffer with him, sharing in this death, so that, somehow, I can experience the resurrection from the dead!
>
> PHILIPPIANS 3:7–11, NLT, EMPHASIS ADDED

More than any other writer, Paul spoke most passionately about knowing Jesus. It was his singular quest in life.

Everything else became peripheral—rubbish—compared to knowing God's Son. And in this text, when he speaks of giving everything up to know Jesus, he uses the Greek word that means *to know by experience*.

But here's the thought that sets me back on my heels. Paul had already experienced Jesus in far more dramatic ways than anyone before or since. On the Damascus highway, Jesus appeared to Paul in a bolt of white fire and spoke to him in person. Sometime later, Paul found himself swept up into the "third heaven," where he had an extended season of personal experience with Jesus.

Yet what did Paul want with all his heart?

He wanted more.

He was still so taken with Jesus that the entire focus of his life was to experience more of Him. Which only proves that once you get a taste, you can never get enough of Him. Having experienced Jesus makes even the brightest treasures of life look dull by comparison.

Do you wonder if this is for you? Wonder no longer! He is at the door of your heart, wanting to come in for some serious fellowship.

Chapter 2

I'D RATHER
HAVE JESUS

If you had to choose between Jesus and something precious to you
…some alluring dream or tantalizing desire…
I wonder, would you choose Him?

The meal was just about finished when I leaned over and asked Billy Graham the question I had hoped to ask him all evening.

Martie and I had been seated next to Dr. Graham at a dinner for the staff and board of his organization. Billy, eighty at the time, was lucid and interesting. Wondering what he would say about his highest joys in life, I asked, "Of all your experiences in ministry, what have you enjoyed most?"

Then (thinking I might help him out a little), I quickly added, "Was it your time spent with presidents and heads of state? Or was it—"

Before I could finish my next sentence, Billy swept his hand across the tablecloth, as if to push my suggestions onto the floor.

"None of that," he said. "By far the greatest joy of my life has been my fellowship with Jesus. Hearing Him speak to me, having Him guide me, sensing His presence with me and His power through me. This has been the highest pleasure of my life!"

It was spontaneous, unscripted, and clearly unrehearsed.

There wasn't even a pause.

With a life full of stellar experiences and worldwide fame behind him, it was simply Jesus who was on his mind and on his heart. His lifelong experience with Jesus had made its mark, and Billy was satisfied.

I found Billy Graham's statement that evening more than convicting. I found it motivating—right to the core of my being. With everything in me, I want what he's experienced. I find my heart saying, *If I make it to eighty, I want to say the same thing.*

Even more so when you consider the story of Chuck Templeton.

"I MISS HIM!"

Templeton's name was practically a household word in evangelical homes in the fifties and sixties. He pastored one of Toronto's leading churches and—along with his close friend Billy Graham—helped found Youth for Christ in Canada. His extraordinary ability to communicate God's Word put him in demand on platforms all over North America.

But I don't remember him for his stellar gifts.

I remember him for his renunciation of the faith.

Evangelicals everywhere were rocked by the news that Chuck Templeton had left his church and renounced all he had previously embraced and proclaimed.

The former preacher went on to fame and fortune. He managed two of Canada's leading newspapers, worked his way into an influential position with the Canadian Broadcasting Company—and even took a run at the prime minister's office.

It had been decades since I'd thought of Chuck Templeton. So imagine my surprise when I noticed he had been interviewed by Lee Strobel in his book, *A Case for Faith*.

After reading Templeton's most recent book, *Farewell to God: My Reasons for Rejecting the Christian Faith*, Strobel caught a plane to Toronto to meet with him. Though eighty-three and in declining health, the former preacher vigorously defended his agnostic rejection of a God who claimed to be love, yet allowed suffering across the world to go unchecked.

Then, toward the end of their time together, Strobel asked Templeton point-blank how he felt about Jesus.

Instantly, the old man softened.

He spoke in adoring terms about Jesus, concluding, "In my view He is the most important human being who has ever existed." Then as his voice began to crack, he haltingly said, *"I...miss...Him!"* With that, Strobel writes, tears flooded Templeton's eyes, and his shoulders bobbed as he wept.

Think of it. Billy Graham and Chuck Templeton, two friends who chose radically different paths through life. And near the end of their journeys, one has found Jesus to be his most prized possession, while the other weeps for having left Him long ago.

TAPPING THE SECRET

Cynics might say that you'd expect someone like Graham to have a close walk with Jesus—and that common, ordinary folk like the rest of us can't expect to get there. But my grandmother had it as well. And she was no Billy Graham.

Born of pioneer stock in Michigan, she married a

frontier farmer and gave birth to her children in a drafty, second-floor corner bedroom at home. She simply kept house for her family, far away from the hustle and bustle of high society. No one but friends and family even knew her name. Yet she had tapped the secret as well.

And so can you.

Stepping into a deepening experience with Jesus is something more than keeping short accounts with sin in our lives. It's beyond that. It is about getting far enough beyond *self* that we can see Him more clearly and desire Him more completely.

Let me explain.

First, so there is no confusion, keeping clear ledgers in our lives is basic to experiencing Christ. As long as there is residual sin in our hearts, there will always be a distance. In His Sermon on the Mount, Jesus said, "Blessed are the pure in heart, for they shall see God" (Matthew 5:8). And the tenses in that pronouncement are not futuristic but present. In other words, if you are not pure in heart today, don't count on experiencing Christ in a compelling way.

It's really not complicated. If there is bitterness, unresolved anger, sensual thoughts and actions, pride, untruthfulness, or slander and gossip in your vocabulary, you're going to feel the distance. Jesus doesn't meet us on those playing fields. He'll meet us there to pull us out of the ditch of our own ways, but He won't stay there with us.

I hope you are in a quiet place where you can put this book down for a moment and think carefully about those things in your life that stand between you and Jesus. Go to your knees and open your life to His divine inspection. Pray as the psalmist prayed,

> Search me, O God, and know my heart;
>> Try me and know my anxious thoughts;
> And see if there be any hurtful way in me,
>> And lead me in the everlasting way.
>
> PSALM 139:23–24

Don't shy away from this. He already knows about your secret thoughts and struggles. He has been grieving the distance between your heart and His. At this very instant, He is waiting for you, His cleansing mercy readily available.

Dealing with our sin is step one. But I have a hunch most of us understand that already. In fact, some of us may feel that we've been making fairly good progress in that regard.

So…why does Jesus still seem so distant?

If anyone's heart had a clean slate, we'd all probably agree that the apostle Paul qualifies for the honor. Yet Paul insists that his pursuit of a deeper experience with Jesus focuses on a distraction far more subtle than obvious sin. As he writes to the Philippians, he makes the case that we can never fully experience Jesus until we stop being absorbed with ourselves.

Chapter 3

ME OR THEE?

At some point in life, we have to come to grips
with whether "He" or "me" is the main feature
of our existence.

"Daddy, are we famous?"

Libby, my seven-year-old, looked up into my eyes.

Famous? I was pastoring a church in a small Midwestern town at the time, and it didn't take me long to respond.

"No, honey," I assured her. "We're not famous at all."

She paused thoughtfully, and then with confidence and a touch of consternation, replied, "Well, we *would* be if more people knew about us."

Poor Libby, only seven, and already concerned with what people thought about us. With whether or not we registered on the Richter scale of public opinion.

It is something that Libby will likely wrestle with the

rest of her life. She, like all of us, will spend her days struggling through the sticky web of self-absorbed perspectives. Since earliest childhood we have been very much aware of and concerned about ourselves. We mastered words like *my* and *mine* long before we knew the word for *friend* or *share*.

Now, as grown-ups, we find ourselves haunted regularly by questions like these: *Who am I? What do people think of me? Have I been sufficiently recognized for my accomplishments? How am I being treated? Does anyone care about me?*

Americans spend millions of dollars trying to get to know themselves. Books about knowing and understanding "who you really are" consistently make the bestseller lists. Obscene amounts of money go to therapists who offer to guide you on a journey through your inner self.

Frankly, can you think of a scarier thought than taking an inner journey through yourself? It's not only a scary thought, it may be an unbiblical one. If you are in the process of becoming a fully devoted follower of Christ, then life is an adventure in getting to know Jesus. And, when we live to know Him, we find that knowing Him is the key to understanding and making peace with ourselves.

Trying to discover self-worth? *You have it in Him....* *He died for you!*

Plagued by failure and guilt? *He does what no one else will or can do for you.... He forgives and forgets, kills the fatted calf as heaven rejoices, and clothes you with the best robes of His righteousness.*

Searching for significance? *Search no more...you are His child. There is no greater significance than that.*

Wondering if there is any reason or purpose for you to take up space on this care-worn planet? *The mystery is unraveled in Him as He scripts your life to be lived for His glory and to reflect the radiance of His character.*

Let's face it, absorption with self is inadequate to satisfy the soul—and completely inept to solve the restless searching of our hearts. Life *must* be about more than getting to know ourselves. Ultimately, self-preoccupation is an empty, boring pursuit. No matter how charming, witty, or profound we may be, we were not created to enthrall ourselves with ourselves for long periods of time.

Simply put, we need Him!

TIRED OF ME

I'm only fifty-seven, and I already find myself weary of the hollow thoughts of what few accomplishments I may have mustered in my life. My failures continue to embarrass me. The inadequacies I have carried with me since my youth still frustrate me. My insecurities still trouble my soul. And the praise of others has an increasingly hollow ring. I am tired of worrying about whether or not the sermon I preached was good enough or whether or not someone will pat me on the back for a job well done. I'm tired of worrying about what people think about me. I'm weary of the carnal feeling that sometimes haunts me when someone talks about his favorite preacher and it's not me.

Bottom line, I just flat out get tired of me. But I never get tired of Jesus.

After all these years, I still find Him more compelling, more engaging, more awesome, more surprising, more fulfilling, and more attractive than ever before.

I never get tired of singing His praises or of watching Him perform. I find Him to be gripping. Absorbing. Beyond comprehension. And that's why—along with Paul, my grandmother, Billy Graham, and countless others through the years—I find myself longing to know Him better.

I am becoming increasingly aware that life doesn't go on forever. When we're young, we think we're bulletproof. We live like we'll never die. But when your knees protest certain movements and your eyesight and memory begin to grow fuzzy, reality sets in. I can see the day coming when there'll be another president of Moody—and a better one at that. There'll be other preachers who bless hungry hearts.

And me? I'll be sitting in the corner of some nursing home waiting for them to ring the lunch bell. And if life up to that point has been all about me, that is going to be a sad and empty day—no matter what they're serving for lunch. Why? Because all I will have will be me! Which at that point won't be much.

But…if my life has been about knowing Jesus and experiencing a deepening relationship with Him, as I sit in that corner of the nursing home waiting for the lunch bell to ring, He'll be there with me.

The mighty Son of God.

The Bright and Morning Star.

The Desire of all Nations.

The Great Shepherd of the sheep.

The wondrous Creator of all.

The King of kings and Lord of lords.

And He'll be more wonderful on that day than ever before. He'll walk with me as I toddle along the linoleum in my walker. He'll talk with me, and I won't have any trouble hearing Him when He tells me that I am His own. He'll say, "Well, Joe, you're almost home." And I'll say, "Lord, the sooner the better. I've heard Your voice through all these years, but I can't wait to see Your face." He and I will be having such a grand time of fellowship, I just might miss that lunch bell.

It's time that we all got real about where Jesus fits in the overall picture of our lives. At some point, the sooner in life the better, we have to come to grips with whether "He" or "me" will be the main feature of our existence. Careful, it's easy to fudge—to think that you can be fully absorbed with yourself and in hot pursuit of Him at the same time. But that isn't reality. You can't have it both ways.

Paul was well aware of the radical choice he would have to make to fully experience the presence and power of Jesus in his life. For him the decision was clear. He chose Jesus.

All right, you say, but he had an edge. After all, he had literally been in the presence of Jesus Christ. Probably twice. I doubt that any of us would be interested in a self-absorbed life if we had actually met the Lord of the universe face-to-face! Fast-food hamburgers lose some of their glow after you've tied into a killer steak!

But in spite of that, he still faced the tension of getting lost in himself. Paul's résumé offered a tempting list of accomplishments that would have seduced the best of us to become fully self-absorbed. Listen to him rattle off his credentials. In the crowd he ran with, this would have been good for some multiple "wows." He writes…

> Yet I could have confidence in myself if anyone could. If others have reason for confidence in their own efforts, I have even more! For I was circumcised when I was eight days old, having been born into a pure-blooded Jewish family that is a branch of the tribe of Benjamin. So I am a real Jew if there ever was one! What's more, I was a member of the

Pharisees, who demand the strictest obedience to the Jewish law. And zealous? Yes, in fact, I harshly persecuted the church. And I obeyed the Jewish law so carefully that I was never accused of any fault.

PHILIPPIANS 3:4–6, NLT

And yet…. And yet his choice is clear….

I once thought all these things were so very important, but now I consider them worthless because of what Christ has done. Yes, everything else is worthless when compared with the priceless gain of knowing Christ Jesus my Lord. I have discarded everything else, counting it all as garbage, so that I may have Christ and become one with him.

VV. 7–9, NLT

Hear his passion…. *You can take all the newspaper clippings, book reviews, and academic honors. Take the prized business card, retirement watch, and bowling trophies and stuff 'em in a Dumpster. They mean less than NOTHING to me compared to Jesus, compared to knowing Him better every day.*

Taking this step doesn't mean that we stop having what we have, doing what we do, or being who we are. It simply means we are no longer consumed by it all. We are consumed instead with Jesus.

As Jesus welcomes us to lose ourselves in Him, He reminds us, "Whoever finds his life will lose it, and whoever loses his life for my sake will find it" (Matthew 10:39, NIV).

What an intriguing thought.

Chapter 4

BLUE RIBBONS

*Beware the danger of losing Jesus
in the glitter of your own goodness.*

What happens—what are the consequences—when followers of Christ forget that Jesus comes first, and get absorbed in themselves and their own accomplishments?

It's never a pretty picture.

My mind jumps back to an incident from junior high days. I remember standing with my buddies in the hall outside our Sunday school room. We were way too cool to get into our chairs early for class. The name of the game was hanging out in the hall to "see and be seen" as all the Sunday foot traffic went by. On this particular Sunday we spotted a visitor—a boy about our age coming down the hall toward our classroom with his mother. Since he was new, we immediately sized him up.

As he came closer, we caught a glimpse of something that clearly marked him. It was bad enough that he was coming with his *mom,* but what was that hanging on the lapel of his suit? Closer examination revealed it to be a long string of Sunday school attendance pins.

In case you didn't grow up in this kind of a church, let me bring you up to speed. If you had perfect attendance in Sunday school for one year, you received a small round metal pin that you could wear, signifying your faithfulness. If you had another perfect year, you won a wreath that went around the pin, with two small loops at the bottom. The loops were for the bars that could be attached year after year to each other if you maintained a spotless attendance record.

This boy must not have missed a Sunday since the day he was born. He looked like a little Russian general, decked out with a chestful of battle ribbons. The bars under his award pin seemed to swing as he walked. In fact, we thought that he tilted a little to the left under the weight of it all.

And what do you think? That we guys in the hallway were blown away by this kid's stellar spiritual accomplishments? That we stood in awe and stunned admiration of his impeccable Sunday school credentials?

No chance.

It was more like, *"Who does this guy think he is?"*

Obviously, it wasn't the most gracious or praiseworthy response, but it came naturally.

This was the essence of the destructive dynamic under way among first-century followers of Jesus in the city of Philippi. And if we're not careful, it easily becomes the ruling pattern in our own lives as well.

THE HOLIER-THAN-THOU CROWD

Any way you look at it, the Judaizers were trouble.

The strident teachings of this group within the early church were more than controversial. They were explosive. Simply put, the Judaizers taught that the death of Christ wasn't enough for salvation. The Lord's sacrifice on the cross did not cancel the requirements of the law and the countless demands of the Levitical system. Therefore, in their view, authentic Christians were to continue to observe sacrifices, circumcision, the Sabbath, and other aspects of the multiplicity of rules handed down by Moses. If you had the Real Deal, you would keep all the requirements of the law.

And guess who thought they were the authentic Christians?

The Judaizers.

As you might imagine, they were rather taken with themselves. They were the "true believers" with the inside scoop on what pleased God.

Never mind that their doctrine flew in the face of the apostles' teaching that Jesus fulfilled all the law and its requirements. According to countless passages in the Epistles, the new covenant in Christ made His work supreme and final—and our good works are simply a reflection of our love and allegiance to Him.

The way the Judaizers saw it, however, they were simply better than the average "loose-living" so-called Christian.

On the other side, the "faith alone" crowd looked at the Judaizers as prime examples of legalism gone amok. As the two camps began to debate, argue, and polarize, they focused on their own distinctives and rejoiced in their own doctrinal correctness.

"We've got it right, and you've got it all wrong."

"No, WE'VE got it right, and YOU'VE got it all wrong."

"No, we don't!"

"Yes, you do!"

And guess who got lost in the scuffle?

Jesus.

That suited Satan's plans perfectly. The church at Philippi was ready to self-destruct—to implode under the weight of its own intramural "Who's the Best?" tournament. The Judaizers were convinced they had won. They kept all the Law. Their work, instead of being a reflection of their love for Jesus, was a reflection of their love for themselves.

It is a strange and subtly destructive dynamic that the better we become, the more we seem to get stuck on ourselves. The demons of pride and self-adulation lurk just around the corner of every good deed. If we're not careful, the better we are, the worse we might become.

Living to flaunt your goodness or to measure yourself by everyone else may very well be the major barrier to a deepening experience of Jesus in our lives. As we have said, life cannot be about you and Him at the same time. Either you are the feature or He is. Take your pick.

In our Christian culture there are lots of fields on which to play this "look-at-me" game....

- Keeping the longest list of rules and living as though strictness is next to godliness
- Serving in high-profile positions in churches and worthy organizations
- Serving in low-profile positions in those same places
- Finding success in the marketplace
- Raising godly kids
- Home-schooling
- Not home-schooling
- Worshiping with contemporary music
- Worshiping in the traditional way
- Using newer Bible translations

- Rejecting newer Bible translations and sticking with the older ones
- Giving large amounts of money
- Getting invitations to the "right" events

The list goes on. And while we don't actually pass out blue ribbons or medals for spiritual accomplishments, we do tend to wear them in our attitudes and self-serving chatter. And when we do, we betray the secret that we've been trying to hide: that life, even when we serve Jesus, is really about "me" after all.

So what is a Jesus seeker to do? Stop being good? Stop being blessed? Stop serving? Stop obeying? Stop sacrificing and surrendering?

Obviously not. Then what are we to do?

Having learned that experiencing Jesus requires transitioning from being self-absorbed, we are now ready to begin the journey toward Him.

Read carefully.

Experiencing Jesus begins with two attitude shifts.

Chapter 5

ON A FENCE POST

Attitude Shift #1…
REJOICE IN THE LORD.

Have you ever been around Christians who smile about everything?

Does it trouble you…just a little?

I must admit, it bothers me. From where I sit, this sort of attitude robs our Christian life of the honest emotions of grief and appropriate anger. It robs us of the healthy emotional swings we experience day by day, hour by hour. It denies the therapy of an uncontrolled belly laugh and the cleansing of a good cry. I'm trying to figure out what these smile machines know that I don't. Maybe they've gotten their signal to be happy all the time from Paul's exhortation to "rejoice in the Lord"—which was buttressed by his follow-up statement to "rejoice in the Lord always;

again I will say, rejoice!" (Philippians 3:1; 4:4).

Thankfully, when Paul opened the third chapter of Philippians with the command to "rejoice in the Lord," he wasn't asking us to go around 24/7 with a praise smile on our face. To expect anybody—much less Christians in the early church who faced excruciating persecution—to be constantly "happy" is something of a stretch.

Besides, biblical joy is never defined as an unending emotional high. Jesus wept over Lazarus, spent a season alone grieving over the brutal murder of His cousin John, and was thoroughly tested in every point even as we are.

So what did Paul mean? Given the problem of the self-inflated Judaizers and the apostle's following statements about the supremacy of knowing Christ, his conclusion is pretty clear.

It's time to stop rejoicing in ourselves and start rejoicing in Jesus. As we have learned, deciding not to be self-absorbed is important. But we will quickly slide back into its grip if we don't replace it with an active and aggressive pattern of rejoicing in Him.

Rejoicing in Jesus is the liberating response that frees us from the endless task of trying to satisfy and fill our souls with ourselves and our accomplishments. It frees us from the endless torment of worrying about being recognized, affirmed, and adequately appreciated. It soothes otherwise fragile egos that are quickly frustrated and irritated when others don't live up to our expectations or when we don't get what we think we "deserve."

Living to brag on Jesus instead of ourselves must have been what Jeremiah had in mind when he declared:

> This is what the LORD says: "Let not the wise man gloat in his wisdom, or the mighty man in his might, or the rich man in his riches. Let them boast in this alone: that they truly know me and understand that I am the LORD who is just and righteous, whose love is unfailing, and that I delight in these things. I, the LORD, have spoken!"
>
> JEREMIAH 9:23–24, NLT

When you think about it, there is far more to brag about in Him than the best of what any of us could ever hope to be or accomplish. When Paul celebrated Christ's awesome list of credentials, he could hardly stop writing for the sheer joy of it all.

He was shamelessly boasting.

He went on and on.

And it felt so right!

Who is Jesus? He's the One:

> …in whom we have redemption, the forgiveness of sins. And He is the image of the invisible God, the first-born of all creation. For by Him all things

were created, both in the heavens and on earth,
visible and invisible, whether thrones or domin-
ions or rulers or authorities—all things have been
created by Him and for Him. And He is before all
things, and in Him all things hold together. He is
also head of the body, the church; and He is the
beginning, the first-born from the dead; so that
He Himself might come to have first place in
everything.

COLOSSIANS 1:14–18

Boasting is a healthy activity when it centers on Jesus.
You can introduce Him to others with as long a string of
superlatives as you want. You can list His accomplishments,
cite His wonderful qualities, talk constantly about His
kindness and mercy and love, and sing His praises for the
rest of your life.

And that would be a good thing to do, because He
deserves it all.

And more.

So why do we keep drawing attention to ourselves?
Why do we want to get the credit and seek applause for our
good deeds? Why do we boast in our accomplishments?
Why do we keep kidding ourselves? Everything good we've
ever managed to do is because of Him, accomplished in and
through His grace and strength. If it weren't for Him—His

grace to save me and supply my life with all I've needed to accomplish and succeed—I would be and do nothing of significance at all.

That isn't modesty or false humility. It's not "Aw, shucks." It's stark reality.

You simply cannot exaggerate when you are speaking of His worth. He belongs in the place of preeminence.

And if in your heart you have become preeminent, then He is not. It bears repeating: Either He is preeminent, or you are. To think that even the best of us can compete with Him is an embarrassing arrogance.

I'm not saying we have nothing to rejoice about in ourselves. Anyone who is anxious to please Christ and who has been gifted and blessed has a lot to feel good about. God doesn't want to deny you the sweet feel of a straight and long golf shot, a tender kiss from one you love, a contract won, an investment that succeeds, or the pleasure of a task superbly performed. Seeking Jesus by living to rejoice in Him does not require you to lapse into self-defacing, nonproductive "woe-is-me-ness."

Nevertheless, if you and I are ever going to experience Jesus in the way we long to experience Him, we need to learn how to get beyond ourselves and our achievements *to get all the way to Him.* We need to cultivate a reflex response that immediately triggers gratefulness and praise to Him for enabling us to accomplish what we do…when something good happens in life…when we've performed well and received a few strokes…when we've been acknowledged and affirmed…when our fondest dreams have come true.

When we are blessed, we need to master the response that takes that spark of joy we feel about ourselves and lets it *explode* into the joy of celebrating His preeminent provision and grace in our lives.

The moment you do this, you connect with Him and lose yourself in His abundant goodness.

UP ON A FENCE POST

A number of years ago, a friend of mine wrote a book he entitled *Turtle on a Fence Post;* it was the story of his highly successful life. What a great title. Stop and think about it: How does a turtle ever make it to the top of a fence post?

He certainly didn't climb there.

If a turtle is on a fence post you can rest assured that someone put him there. It took a power beyond his own to place him on that lofty perch. And when you answer the question of how you got to the top of *your* fence post, then you'll be ready to turn from celebrating yourself and begin to celebrate Him.

Resisting the ever-present tendency to rejoice in our

own preeminence demands that we learn to recognize when we are tangled in its web. Do you know what those tacky strands of webbing feel like?

- Is it your knee-jerk reaction to take credit for your accomplishments, or do you instinctively recognize and rejoice in His grace in all that you have and do?
- Are you bothered or—worse yet—bitter about the times you have been slighted, and your rights and privileges have not been respected?
- Have you ever performed for the praise of others?
- Are you prone to complain that you don't have all that you deserve, and compare yourself in self-pity to others who have more?
- Is church (really) about *you* and *your* preferences?

If this is your profile, then it should be clear why Jesus and a deepening experience with Him is at best a vague notion on your spiritual wish list. But when we live to praise Him for all that He is and master the liberating art of celebrating His worthiness rather than our own, we have positioned ourselves to meet Him in a way beyond what we have ever experienced before. And it is important to note that this principle needs to be operative in bad times as well as good.

I'm reminded of Paul's arresting comment that he had

learned how to be content in both "want" as well as "pros-perity" (Philippians 4:12). In "want" we rarely think about "rejoicing in the Lord." We usually spend great amounts of time fretting and feeling sorry for ourselves. We torment ourselves with a sense of being cheated out of the comfort, health, wealth, and happiness we think we deserve.

With that attitude, life is still totally about me. Big-time. And while a little dose of that feels good for a brief moment, we can't stay there. We've got to turn the corner. Rejoicing in the Lord in bad times means learning to give thanks in everything (1 Thessalonians 5:18). It means that we rejoice in the fact that a wise God gives and takes away, and we bless the name of the Lord (Job 1:21). That we are truly rich in Him even if we are poor in this world's goods (Revelation 2:9). That He never leaves us or forsakes us (Hebrews 13:5–6). That He works all things together for good (Romans 8:28). That in our weakness He is made strong and that His grace is abundantly sufficient (2 Corinthians 12:7–10). That it is by His wise and over-seeing permission that we have been placed on the fence post of trouble, and that through the darkest of trials He can bring glory and good.

We have not learned how to live in pain or prosperity until we have learned how to use them as a springboard to a life of grateful praise and adoration to our Lord.

Do you really believe that whatever benefits you receive from the hand of God flow only from His grace and are completely undeserved?

Are you convinced that even in the darkest of times He is with you, that He has a purpose, and that He will not waste your sorrows?

If you answer yes to these questions, you're on your way to a closer walk with the Son of God. The psalmist tells us that He inhabits the praises of His people (Psalm 22:3, KJV). Strangely enough, it doesn't say that He inhabits our complaints or our self-serving compliments. If your heart is full of complaining or self-pity—or of self-congratulating applause—you won't experience His nearness. Positioning our lives to experience Jesus requires seeing beyond the blessings and burdens of life...to fill our hearts with Him alone. In the process, we learn the sweet skill of boasting on Him, regardless.

He inhabits the praises of His people.

Meet Him there.

Chapter 6

THE GREATEST VALUE

Attitude Shift #2…
VALUE JESUS ABOVE EVERYTHING.

Think for a minute about the things you've treasured in your life.

At age one or two, it might have been a raggy, bedraggled baby blanket that you clung to like life itself. Woe unto the person who attempted to remove it from your grasp!

At age three or four, maybe it was a stuffed animal or doll that somehow became as real and as important to you as anything else in your world.

By six or seven, it might have been that first bike. You wouldn't have traded it for anything. Maybe you had a little collection of some kind tucked away in one of your dresser drawers, or in a shoe box under your bed…pretty rocks or dolls or comic books or baseball cards or stickers or those tiny green plastic army men.

As the years rolled along, it might have been some wonderful experience you wanted to hold onto…a winning hit at a Little League game…an A on one of your papers…a lead in the school play…an invitation to join an honor society…a date with one of those cute cheerleaders or the big man on campus.

At one point in time, those things were very precious to you. You protected them and pondered them and held them tightly in your memory. They gave you delight and pleasure. They made you feel warm all over again.

But where are they now? Life goes on, doesn't it? And we move on to encounter new and more intriguing possessions and experiences. Our picture albums, basements, attics, and garages are a living testimony to the changing values in our lives.

A CHAOS OF PRICE TAGS

You may have heard the story about the pranksters who broke into a hardware store. Strangely enough, they didn't steal a thing. Yet what they did created chaos of epic proportions.

They switched all the price tags.

The proprietor was unaware of anything amiss until the first customer stepped to the cash register with a claw hammer. And it rang up at $199.95. Naturally, the customer's jaw dropped. "What's that thing made out of?" he demanded. "Platinum?"

On further inspection, employees noticed that a big screen TV in the appliance section was selling for $14.95. The goods were all the same, resting on the same shelves as the night before, but the assigned values were hopelessly jumbled.

We are so prone to do that with our lives. More often than not we assign the wrong value to who we are and what we have.

The apostle Paul had the price tags right....

The very credentials these people are waving around as something special, I'm tearing up and throwing out with the trash—along with everything else I used to take credit for. And why? Because of Christ. Yes, all the things I once thought were so important are gone from my life. Compared to the high privilege of knowing Christ Jesus as my Master, firsthand, everything I once thought I had going for me is insignificant—dog dung. I've dumped it all in the trash so that I could embrace Christ and be embraced by him.... I gave up all that inferior stuff so I could know Christ personally.

PHILIPPIANS 3:7–8, 10, *THE MESSAGE*

There's Paul at the cash register, looking at all the price tags attached to his experiences, accomplishments, and treasures. He's got a red pen in his hand, and all those things that used to be so valuable, so precious, so terribly important to Paul, have been slashed down to zero. In fact, he's loading them up in boxes, headed for the Dumpster out back.

And what about knowing Jesus—the name Paul used to hate and assigned no value to at all? He can't even put a price on the privilege of experiencing Him. He writes Beyond Price on the tag because there's no way he can even describe how precious it is to him.

I'm reminded of a friend of ours who was an avid decorator. She had all the knack and instinct to make a room come alive. Then, in the midst of one of her decorating sprees, the doctor told her she had cancer. To that point her decorating project had her in its grip. She woke up with it every morning and fell asleep rearranging the details. Her day was consumed with fabric swatches and catalogs strewn around the house.

But on that day that she drove home from her doctor's office, the joy and fixation with that decorating project evaporated like water on a Phoenix sidewalk. Just that quickly, *life itself* had become precious. So precious that everything else that used to bring her joy was insignificant.

How often have you heard it?

—A widower lamenting over the misplaced values that robbed him of precious time with his wife.

—A dad who had valued life at the office more than time at home with his young son.

—A working mom who treasured a promotion at work more than watching her baby girl grow up.

—A retiree who spent money carelessly through his working years and had nothing left for retirement.

Getting our values straight is a critically important issue in life. And it is particularly strategic for the one seeking to experience Jesus.

In my limited experience, I've noticed two kinds of shoppers: those who check the contents listed on the side of the box for value, and those who like how the box looks. My wife, Martie, is a value shopper. She reads every label, right down to the tiny print. She compares weight to price per ounce, and when she finally throws it in the cart you can count on the fact that she has nabbed the best value.

If you value what looks good and gives you a buzz, then your heart will embrace all that is temporal and seductive. But if you look hard and long at Jesus, if you read all that the label says about His matchless worth, then Christ will have your heart. Every time. All the time.

Perhaps you've never thought of contrasting what you

value most with how you value Christ. But to experience Him in the fullness He intends, you've got to go through the exercise. And this exercise is far more than just giving mental assent to the fact that Jesus is most important. Most of us have been doing that all of our lives—and then go on to live like He was eighth or ninth on the list. *It's only when we understand why there is no one like Him and nothing else besides Him that we are able to embrace His unsurpassable value—even in the face of the fiercest of competitors.*

READ THE LABEL

Our attitude change regarding what is most important to us has to be more than "church-speak." There needs to be irrefutable substance to the claim. What is the proof of His supreme value? What is it about Him that would convince our hearts that compared to Him everything else in our life is like rubbish?

There are three all-surpassing realities that Jesus brings to our life that no one else—indeed, nothing else—even hopes to offer. These qualities ascribe unprecedented value to Christ. It is these three that gripped the apostle heart like a vise, that by comparison left the apostle counting everything else in his life as loss.

It all started at the Cross.

1. It is at the Cross that we "gain" Christ (Philippians 3:8).

If "gaining" Jesus is of substantive value, then what is it that we gain? Simply put, if you gain Him, you have all you need. Most importantly, gaining Him means gaining total and eternal forgiveness for all your sins and shortcomings—past, present, and future. There is nothing on earth that can compete with the gift of His saving grace. And the astounding reality is that *anyone* who repentantly comes to Jesus receives the irrevocable privilege of gaining Him.

One of my all-time favorite stories from the Gospels is in Luke 12. It's the account of the man who was indignant and troubled by the fact that his brother had cheated him out of his inheritance. One day, he happened to find himself in the presence of Jesus, the Nazarene. He caught the Lord's attention and complained, "Master, tell my brother to divide the inheritance with me!"

As with so many who spoke with Jesus, he got more than he bargained for in the answer. The Lord replied, "Watch out! Be on your guard against all kinds of greed; a man's life does not consist in the abundance of his possessions" (Luke 12:15, NIV). Jesus went on to tell the story of a rich and successful farmer. This man had been blessed with such a great harvest that he had to tear down all his little barns and build big ones just to store his bumper crop of grain. Inviting his friends to celebrate his good fortune, the wealthy man apparently left someone off the invitation list.

It was God.

But He showed up anyway.

On that very night God required the wealthy farmer's soul, and all of those carefully hoarded goods went to someone else. Jesus didn't mince words about the barn-building man. He called him a fool. Not because he had been so successful, not because he had so much stuff, but because he valued it as his ultimate security and placed no value on God in his life. As Jesus said on another occasion, "What will it profit a man if he gains the whole world and forfeits his soul?" (Matthew 16:26).

Bottom line? Without Jesus, all the goods and gear and gadgets this consumer culture can throw at us are just so many cheap toys; all the success in the world is of no ultimate value at all. Gaining Jesus not only settles the problem of guilt and judgment before a just and holy God, but it also showers us with an abundance of other graces with which nothing in this world can compete.

—An incomparably rich inheritance reserved for you, that no government can tax, no thief can plunder, no terrorist can explode, and no temperamental rich uncle can revoke.

—Our Lord's 24/7/365 presence, so that you have nothing to fear from man, woman, angel, or demon.

—An Advocate in heaven who sticks up for you and

pleads your case when the devil hurls accusations against you.

—A limitless supply of grace to help you in the time of need...and countless other unparalleled advantages.

2. At the Cross we are placed "in Him" (Philippians 3:9).

When we came to the Cross we not only gained Him, we entered into the privilege of being found "in Him." This is a concept so big that it's hard to bend our minds around it. As Paul notes, being found in Him means that you and I have been wrapped in the very righteousness of Jesus Christ. Try to imagine the blinding, searing, white fire at the core of a new star blazing in the heavens. Now...what if you could take that searing radiance and just slip it over your shoulders like a robe?

That just begins to describe what it means to have the righteousness of Jesus—the perfect, sinless, spotless Lamb of God—covering all of your life.

Apart from "being found in Him," we could not approach the throne of God in prayer. We could not draw near to the majestic presence of our God without being instantly vaporized. But covered in our Lord's own righteousness, we can approach a holy God with confidence and worship Him without fear. We can share our deepest thoughts and longings, knowing that He hears and cares. And we can find grace and mercy to help us in our time of need.

In the midst of a hostile and often intimidating world, He clothes us with His own robe and guarantees our safety all the way home. To put it plainly, Jesus has you covered. As my street friends say, He's got your back! And in a relationship with a holy God, that's a very big deal!

3. Having Jesus and being found in Him guarantees our resurrection from the dead (Philippians 3:11).

By far the most popular notion today regarding life after death is reincarnation. For the life of me, I can't understand why anyone would want to come back and go through the disaster of another lifetime. But if you don't have God's Word, then all you have is the hope of some vague human recycling project.

The next stop after death is not a recycled life in a different body; it is accountability for what I have done in life, and for what I have done with Jesus and His offer of eternal life. As God's Word says, "It is appointed for men to die once and after this comes judgment" (Hebrews 9:27). But in Jesus we no longer fear that judgment day. Jesus has clearly said, "I am the resurrection and the life; he who believes in Me will live even if he dies, and everyone who lives and believes in Me will never die" (John 11:25–26).

Think of it. A pass in Him at the judgment, all that is "far better" throughout eternity, and in the darkest of days here on earth, the bright hope of an eternity of sorrowless joy. In Jesus we boisterously and with great confidence sing, "O DEATH, WHERE IS YOUR VICTORY? O DEATH, WHERE IS YOUR STING?... Thanks be to God, who gives us the victory through our Lord Jesus Christ" (1 Corinthians 15:55, 57).

UNSURPASSED VALUE

So tell me.

    Is there anything you have

        anything you might hope to have

            anything you are or hope to become

                that can compare with Jesus?

Is there anyone else to whom you are more gratefully indebted? Is there a reason—any reason at all—why He would not be more highly prized in your life than anything else or anyone else?

Think back to the day when you invited Jesus into your life as Savior and Lord. In order to receive this triple-grace-bestowed benefit we just spoke of, you had to leave all that you were and had at the foot of the cross and come with no merit of your own. Remember?

You had to tear up your list of accomplishments.

Burn your journal of good deeds.

Shred your file of newspaper clippings.

Why? Because the cross is all about Christ and Christ alone.

This is exactly the point that Paul is making. In order to gain Christ, in order to be found in Him, in order to experience resurrection from the dead, Paul had to count all things loss for the exceeding value of knowing Jesus. And so did you. It was there, at the foot of His cross, that you laid all your trophies down so that you could gain Jesus.

God has never looked at a portfolio of greatness, turned to Peter (who for some reason is always at heaven's gate), and said, "Check this out! Can you believe we get someone of this caliber as a resident in heaven? Unlock the gate! This one's a keeper!" Quite the contrary. As Scripture says, we are saved by grace through faith, and it is not of ourselves. It is a gift of God. It is not of works, because if that were so, we would spend eternity boasting about ourselves (see Ephesians 2:8–9).

It is at the cross, then, that we put all our blue ribbons and trophies in a pile. We stand as it were naked before Him, pleading His mercy and grace. And instead of judging us, He touches us with His love, makes us His own, clothes us with His own perfect righteousness, and guarantees our resurrection on that final day.

Before the cross, all the value is affixed to us—all we are and have. At the cross, He alone is of supreme value.

So why, after receiving all that we have in Christ, do we dig those old trophies out of the trash heap? When did we stop clinging to the cross and start valuing our own merit again? How ludicrous, how deeply offensive it must be to Jesus when we reach back and reclaim what we gladly forfeited to gain Him—as though it were now of greater value to us again. Was He of supreme value only for the moment of salvation? Of course not. We need Him every hour of the day, with every breath we draw into our lungs.

Keep your eyes on Jesus.

Stay at the cross every day.

Remember the mercy and grace that freely flowed to cover you.

Cling to its blood-stained timbers.

Lose yourself in the glory of His amazing grace.

If you do, it won't be long until you've put "self" in its proper place—and Jesus in His.

When our attitudes have shifted to move self out of the way, and to value Jesus more highly than anything we are or have, we are ready to experience Jesus in three "meeting places." He meets us in the seductions of life, in the midst of our suffering, and in the process of full surrender. These may not be places where you thought He would be.

But He is there just the same.

And He is waiting for you.

Chapter 7

DELIVER US FROM EVIL

Experiencing Jesus in seasons of seduction.

Temptations. All of us have them. It shouldn't be hard to think of the last time you were caught in the tension of a choice between good and evil—or even something good and not so good.

How easy to utter a quick lie, just a little one, to get off the hook.

To let an offense take us all the way to a shouting match or brawl.

To let our minds become an incubator for irritations that turn into angry words and hurtful schemes of revenge. Or a playground where fantasies burrow in and begin expressing themselves in attitudes and actions.

Temptations are everywhere. They show up in moments of victory, and they leer at us in the midst of despair. They dress like money, wear fine perfume and rich cologne, go high tech on the Internet, make anger seem sweet, and offer bitterness as a five-star luxury. Temptations lure us to give in to our doubts and to live for what seems right at the moment. They love what feels good. In short, they offer the sizzle of sin…for a season.

But for all we know about temptation, few of us have imagined that we can experience Jesus in its midst. After all, He's the sinless one. He's the one who taught us to pray, "Lead us not into temptation…." Temptation? That's Satan's territory!

Nevertheless, it's true. Temptation is one of the places where we can experience a fresh closeness with our Lord. And given the frequency of temptations in our lives, it becomes an opportunity to meet Him on a regular basis!

In a moment we will explain—or should I say, let's have Paul explain what he means when he writes "…that I may know Him and the power of His resurrection" (Philippians 3:10). But first, it's important to put meeting Jesus in times of temptation into the bigger picture of what Paul is saying.

To this point in the text, Paul has reveled in what theologians would call the *positional* blessings that we have in Jesus. If we have been to the cross, we are in the privileged *position* of having gained Christ, of being found in Him, and of being guaranteed a part in the resurrection from the dead (vv. 8–9, 11). Positional blessings are prized realities secured for us *no matter what* through the grace of His work at Calvary. Unfortunately many followers of Jesus are content to bask in what we have in Jesus without actually experiencing Jesus.

Paul, however, isn't satisfied to simply bask in these "positional" gifts. He makes it clear that gaining Jesus and being found in Him are actually intended to enable us to enjoy a real-life, day-by-day experience with Jesus.

When Paul begins verse 10 with "that I may know Him," he uses a "purpose clause." Simply put, we gain Christ and are found in Him *for the purpose* of having an experiential relationship with Him. To revel in those positional privileges without going on to experience Jesus is to abort the very purpose of the gifts!

I have a friend here in Chicago who owns a company that has skyboxes for the Cubs, the White Sox, and the Bulls. In fact, he has front row, center court, feet-on-the-playing-floor tickets for all of the Bulls games. In the Michael Jordan era, Bulls tickets were the most coveted commodities in town (my how the mighty have fallen!). Every year, believe it or not, I get a shot at these tickets. And what can I say? It's wonderful. Experiencing the Cubs at Wrigley Field from the luxurious confines of a skybox or feeling the breeze generated when giant NBA players run past you at the United Center is a super-charged experience for an unrepentant sports fan.

My friend does all he can to ensure that experience for me. He checks with my schedule and sends me the tickets (sometimes with parking passes); then he'll call me and ask how I enjoyed the game. Good buddy that he is, my friend wants to know that I not only have the tickets in my hand, but that I actually show up at the game, sit in those prime seats, and revel in the experience.

How much sense would it make if I held those tickets—flashing them around and impressing everyone with my opportunity—but decided to skip the game? Not only would I be cheating myself out of a choice experience, I would be embarrassed to see my friend, lest he should ask how I liked the game. Wasting his gracious provision would be unthinkable.

It's a similar situation—only infinitely more serious—if we waste the phenomenal price that Jesus paid that we might enjoy a close and personal relationship with Him. So what's the secret? How do we activate this kind of relationship? Paul tells us we must meet Jesus in three places:

—in the power of His resurrection
—in the fellowship of His sufferings
—and in conformity to the image of His death.

Let's figure out how we encounter Jesus in that first meeting place—resurrection power.

THE FIRST MEETING PLACE...
Experiencing Jesus in His Resurrection Power

You might say that Paul was power hungry. But in this case it was a good thing. God wants you and me to be power hungry, too. He wants to infect us with a deep longing, insatiable hunger, and overpowering desire for power.

But not just any power. If we are hungering and thirsting for the resurrection power of Jesus Christ, we're on the road to experiencing Him in a deeper way. And believe it or not, the resurrection power of Jesus Christ is most frequently experienced in times of temptation.

It may be a little hard to get a grip on this thought because we tend to think of the Resurrection as a glorious future event. And it is certainly that. The power of the Resurrection will kick-start an eternity of unhindered joy in our fellowship with Jesus.

And that, my friend, is a power worth having.

I recall D. James Kennedy preaching about the miracle of the Resurrection. In his sermon he referenced the unfortunate turn of events for Roger Williams, the founder of Rhode Island. He was buried in a rather common setting, which led his admirers several years later to get permission to exhume his body for a burial more appropriate to their hero's image. Imagine their consternation to discover that the roots of a nearby apple tree had worked their way into the casket.

I remember Dr. Kennedy's question at that point. "What now of Roger Williams?" Or of the apples that grew. Or of the people that ate the apple pies made of apples from the tree. Or of those who had eaten the pie and were lost at sea and eaten by sharks? Just think of the miraculous power required to reassemble Roger Williams!

But the real power of the Resurrection lies in its spiritual significance—for what it accomplished in realms far more strategic than the reassembly of scattered remains.

The Resurrection is at its very essence the ultimate victory over sin, death, and hell. All the forces of evil spent their best efforts to permanently ground their Archenemy behind a massive, immovable stone—guarded by imperial guards from the most powerful empire on earth. And then, with a word from God—the merest breath—death was defeated, and sin and the forces of hell no longer held sway. Jesus lives and in Him the power of sin is rendered weak and ineffective.

This is the real power of the Resurrection. And it was hunger for this power that became a mighty longing within the heart of Paul. In it and through it, the apostle tells us, we get to experience Jesus Christ in a deeper way than we've known before.

While it is true that Jesus taught us to pray that He would not lead us into temptation, it is also true that He taught us to pray that God would deliver us from evil.

He waits in every temptation to meet you there. To take you by the hand and deliver you from the hammer blows of the hooded tormentor who lurks just behind the lure of it all.

When was the last time you looked for Jesus in the midst of a pressing temptation? Our problem is that we haven't known He is there! Most of the time we try to break the spell of sin on our own power by learning to fear the consequences, by trying to "buck up" and be good, by finding an accountability partner, or by a dozen other good but inadequate mechanisms.

But only He can deliver you.

Temptation is not foreign to Him. In the wilderness, exhausted and hungry from an extended fast, the King of creation went one-on-one with the great seducer. Jesus is no stranger to our struggles. Which is precisely why Scripture reminds us that He was tempted in every way like we are. He understands and promises to give us grace and mercy to help in our time of need (Hebrews 4:14–16).

Every temptation is a choice. A choice to satisfy our own fallen desires or to satisfy Jesus. *And He is there*—right in that crisis of choice. Learn to look for Him in the very moment that temptation moves in on your desires. And weigh the choice. He always offers something of greater value than the lure being trolled through the waters of your heart.

Need to lie to avoid a problem? Give your problem to Him. *He will help you through, and the truth you tell will reward your heart with the freedom of a clear conscience.*

Feel like cheating to get some extra cash? *He will meet all your needs—miraculously, if necessary.*

Attracted by the buzz of some sensual fulfillment? *He offers the long-term pleasure of a pure heart without damaging and polluting your soul.*

Feel the need to manipulate your way through a problem? *Simply do what is right. He will guide your footsteps and clear the way.*

With every choice you make for Him, you will have met Him there and tasted His resurrection power in your life. And as He delivers you from evil, the purity in your life will open your heart's door to increasingly sweet fellowship with Him.

A listener to our radio program, *Proclaim!*, wrote of his struggle to break the spell that Internet pornography had over his heart. He knew that with every click he was denying and distancing himself from Jesus. To remind him of the choice, he finally put a picture of Jesus in the corner of his computer screen. With that reminder of the presence of Jesus, he found it impossible to pursue those alluring sights.

In the end, most sin is about enhancing or preserving your life, reputation, pleasure, prosperity, or safety. If life is about you, sin will come easily. But if you have begun to live to rejoice in the Lord instead of in yourself, you'll be glad to meet Him in temptation and let Him take you by the hand. If you value Jesus as the preeminent value of your existence, you will never dream of trading Him for the poison porridge of hell.

As you probably know, songs have a way of starting in your head in the morning and staying with you all day. Recently I woke up singing a favorite song from years past, "I'd rather have Jesus…than be held in sin's dread sway." Throughout the day, as temptations ambushed my heart, the words drove me to Him.

I sing that song in my heart a lot these days! It helps me to meet Jesus in times of temptation and to keep my heart pure and open for the One who seeks to come in and dine.

Chapter 8

THE TROUBLE
WITH INTIMACY

Experiencing Jesus in seasons of suffering.

The transatlantic connection was filled with static, but the sound of a broken heart on the other end of the line was all too clear. It was Craig's wife, Martha. As she spoke, everything inside me felt crushed.

Craig and I grew up together. We attended the same college, played soccer together, and in fact looked so much alike that we were often mistaken for brothers. He married a pretty coed in college and after graduation enlisted in the Air Force.

I hadn't seen Craig in years. Imagine my surprise when our paths crossed in the town where I began my first pastorate. Talk had it that Craig and Martha had been far from the Lord. When Martie and I heard that they had recommitted their lives to the Lord, we were overjoyed. It wasn't long before they became active in our little church. He taught our high school boys, and Martha taught the girls. Before long, God led them to work with troubled teens on the island of Haiti.

They'd been in Haiti only a week, and now Martha was telling me that Craig had suffered a serious injury while diving into a pool. He didn't make it through the night. Martha was there alone. Less than thirty years old, and already a widow. Her dreams and hopes dashed. How could this be? Only days into a fresh commitment to serve Jesus, and nothing left to show for it but unbearable loss.

THE TROUBLE WITH TROUBLE

Job's comforters may not have had a lot right, but Eliphaz certainly had a point.

"Man," he said, "is born to trouble as surely as sparks fly upward" (Job 5:7, NIV).

Let's face it: Trouble happens. In fact, as a friend of mine points out, if we really understood the depth of the Fall and the grip that sin has on this world, we would be surprised that anything good happens *at all.*

The trouble with trouble is that it seems so indiscriminate.

Good people suffer. Bad people prosper. Exploiters exploit with seeming impunity. Children are victimized by crack addict parents, and elderly folks end up being neglected and marginalized.

We have a wonderful neighbor in her eighties. Charmingly crusty, with an engaging personality, she seems to enjoy being a touch out-of-sorts about some things. It's her "gig," and we love her for it. She claims that her everyday consumption of gin and cigarettes "keeps her fresh." Her sister, on the other hand, is as proper as they come. She doesn't drink or smoke. She exercises faithfully at the local pool, and she complains about nothing. Last winter, while swimming her daily routine, she was taken ill and lay in a coma in the hospital for days, until she finally died.

Our neighbor was stunned. Her sister was her only living relative. All she could say in the days following her sister's death was, "I don't understand it. *It should have been me!* My sister was such a good person."

The truth, of course, is that none of us is exempt. Jesus stated very clearly, "In this world you will have trouble" (John 16:33, NIV). And He was talking to His closest friends!

Is there anyone left on the planet who actually feels that the world is gradually getting better and better? That we are more civilized? If you harbor such thoughts, consider the horrific events surrounding September 11, 2001—or just spend a few minutes with CNN on any given night.

The good news in all this bad news is that a special experience with Jesus is there for the taking—right in the middle of that hardship.

THE SECOND MEETING PLACE...
Experiencing Jesus in the Fellowship of His Sufferings

Our instincts tell us to resist trouble. To fight it. To resent it as an intruder. To feel cheated. To tell ourselves, *I deserve better than this.* And as those thoughts settle in, the great scramble begins. We plot, manipulate, fret, seek revenge, doubt God and His goodness, threaten, harbor anger, flirt with bitterness, withdraw, and—if all else fails—throw a major pity party. And by the way, if you throw a pity party don't bother sending out invitations. Friends may try to cheer you up—and that would wreck everything.

Thankfully, for those of us who seek the face of God in the midst of trouble, we discover that He is not surprised by the arrival of pain—and that He wants us to experience Him there.

Paul knew that in suffering he had the opportunity to gain a deeper, more experiential knowledge of Jesus. We discover the same thing—that closer, sweeter walk—when we connect with Him in our seasons of suffering. As Paul puts it, there is a special encounter with Christ when we share in the "fellowship of His sufferings" (Philippians 3:10).

If you are thinking here of the Cross, then you will struggle to meet Him in your sufferings. Most likely, none of us will be crucified—not literally. But the sufferings of Christ are far more extensive, more identifiable, than only the injustices of Golgotha.

Have you ever felt lonely, displaced, misrepresented, or misunderstood? Have you ever found yourself severely restricted? Denied of your rights and privileges? Betrayed by a close friend? Have you ever been left out of the power group and plotted against? Have you ever done right and suffered for it? Have you ever tasted the bitterness of injustice? Have you ever longed for your friends to stand with you in your moment of need, only to sense they're really too consumed with their own needs to pay much attention? Have you ever experienced unbearable pain? Have you ever felt abandoned by God?

These, and many more, are the sufferings Jesus endured on our behalf. He bore them in love, patiently and willingly for us, so that "by His stripes, we are healed."

If you found yourself nodding your head to any of those questions, you can identify with what He felt and suffered for you.

The question is not Are you willing to suffer? We have little choice about that. The real question is, Are you willing to meet Jesus there—right in the midst of your pain?

Are you willing to make that choice?

To experience Him in the midst of our pain requires that we stop whining about our trials. How often do we find our hearts complaining, *Why is He doing this to me? Does He really care? Does He truly feel the ache in my heart and the anguish in my spirit? Does He have any idea what He's putting me through?* Residual anger, revenge, bitterness, self-imposed depression, and despair are the rewards we reap from these attitudes.

Jesus has something better in mind.

If we really desire to experience Him, we need to stop blaming God, reverse our self-centered demand for release, and realize for the first time in our lives that we are getting a firsthand experience of what He felt and experienced as He suffered for us. Stop and identify the type of trouble you feel. Think through Christ's suffering and identify where His pain meets yours. Ask Him to forgive you for feeling that you should be exempt. And as you feel His pain in yours, thank Him that He loved you enough to suffer like this for you.

Stay there with Him. Refuse to let Satan draw you back into bitterness and self-pity, and you will find Jesus a meaningful companion in the midst of trouble.

We need to be deeply taken with the thought that in suffering we understand a little of what He went through for us. And maybe, just maybe, we will begin to grasp—

sand particle by sand particle—the depth of His love for us. What words cannot express in trying to explain the marvelous love of Jesus, suffering servants feel in the deepest parts of their souls.

This is the fellowship of His sufferings.

This is the intimacy of a shared experience with Jesus.

This is where He waits to meet us. It's time to stop turning our backs on Him in pain and flee to His embrace.

But we are only free to do this when we have ceased to live to rejoice in ourselves. If we are intent to celebrate "me" in life, we will resist trials and quickly become embittered when they settle in for the long haul—to say nothing of the difficulty in meeting Jesus in pain when we have valued comfort and peace more than nearness to Him. If He is the supreme value in our lives then we will be willing to meet Him in times of trouble.

SHARED EXPERIENCES

Moody has a policy that I do not travel alone. When our children were at home, I often traveled with a colleague from the Institute. After I returned home, I would reenter Martie's world of runny noses, school lunches, taxi runs, and bedtime stories.

I'd try my best to brief her on the trip and tell her about all the things I had seen and the people I had met, but there really wasn't much connection. How could there be? For one thing, I'm a man. And most men like to cut to the bottom line, rather than share details. For another thing, she simply hadn't been there. After I would give my little spiel, she in turn would try to explain to me all that happened while I was gone—all the little trials and joys of caring for growing children. I did my best to enter into her experiences.

But I really couldn't. I hadn't been there.

Now, however, our children are married and have homes of their own. Happily, Martie and I often travel together. We share the experiences of new places and new faces, of sometimes stressful meetings; we watch the Lord work through the ministry of His Word and experience the joy of His work together. We experience missed connections and delightful conversation with new friends around a dinner table in some cozy restaurant.

We come home and talk about where we've been and what we've done. We relive our experiences, smile together over the funny moments, and sigh over the stories of pain and heartache we encounter along the way. It's amazing how much closer we are today in our intimacy with one another. All because of shared experiences. Our lives are no longer two worlds that periodically merge. Our worlds are the same, and we know each other better today than ever before. And we love it this way!

It's like that in our relationship with Jesus. You've got to capitalize on where your world merges with His. And suffering is one of the places where your world and His intersect. If you choose to see your season of suffering as a moment to capture a shared experience with God's Son, your intimacy with Him will become a deepening reality. It is a firsthand experience with the reality of His love for you and the heavy price He paid for your redemption.

Yes, your pain will still be pain—sometimes extremely difficult to endure. But instead of focusing on the loss, the hardship, the obstacle, you will step through the door of a fellowship beyond words to describe.

After Craig's tragic death, questions plagued us all. Why, God? Why now? Why them? But God's grace was strengthening Martha's heart. In the midst of her hurt she chose to see the suffering as a shared experience with Jesus. She wrote to me that she had decided to view her pain through His loss at the Cross. She marked the loneliness and despair in her heart, recalling the loneliness and despair Jesus had experienced for her. His words, "My God, why have You forsaken me?" echoed in her soul. She found solace in Jesus' confidence that His loss was not in vain but that His suffering was a part of His Father's wise and bigger plan. She chose to endure the pain for the joy that was set before her, just as Jesus did (Hebrews 12).

Martha found unusual supporting grace in meeting

Jesus in her loss, and it opened the door of her heart to His strong and abiding presence. Recently she wrote in reflection: "During that time of emotional recovery, God revealed Himself in ways I could not imagine. Physical, financial, emotional, and spiritual needs were met in dramatic and supernatural ways."

Today, Martha teaches a large women's Bible class, has a ministry to women in prison, and has a son who serves as a missionary. Had she not met Jesus in her sorrow, I wonder where lesser instincts might have taken her?

Chapter 9

SWEET SURRENDER

Going all the way to Gethsemane.

Bob always said he wanted a closer walk with the Lord, but seemed continually frustrated. No matter what he did, his longing for Jesus never seemed satisfied.

His pastor had told him he couldn't really expect such a relationship this side of heaven. But Bob knew in his heart there had to be more, more than he was experiencing. What really frustrated him was that others seemed to find that closer, more intimate walk he wanted so much. So he knew it was possible. In fact, he tried so hard that at times he felt frustrated with God. He often thought that if God was truly "a rewarder of those who diligently seek Him," then He must have run out of rewards when Bob stepped up.

He tithed and then some.

He served as an elder in his church.

He regularly met with God in devotions and prayer.

He was good to his wife and spent time with his kids.

He even fasted on occasion.

What else was there to do? What, pray tell, did God expect? What did He require anyway?

Listening to Bob's complaint reminds me of the time that Israel felt the same way. In the days of the prophet Micah they filed a grievance with heaven; in fact, their whole tone seems to indicate that they were miffed about the distance God seemed to keep between Himself and them.

> With what shall I come to the LORD
>> And bow myself before the God on high?
> Shall I come to Him with burnt offerings,
>> With yearling calves?
> Does the LORD take delight in thousands of rams,
>> In ten thousand rivers of oil?
> Shall I present my firstborn for my rebellious acts,
>> The fruit of my body for the sin of my soul?
>
> MICAH 6:6–7

You can almost feel their frustration in the text. *What's it all about, Lord? What does it really take to sense Your nearness? Have we missed something?*

The Lord graciously responded with a reminder of what it is that He requires. He named three keys to closing the distance. (I've always been thankful that our God is a God of short lists. Imagine if He had dropped a tome of detailed requirements for us to live up to. Given His holiness, He could have done just that. But He didn't.) What is it that pleases Him? To do justice. To love mercy. To walk humbly with your God.

It was the "walk humbly with your God" that Bob had unknowingly missed. One of the basic expressions of humility is complete obedience at any cost. When I say no to God, keep an area of my life to myself, or withhold what He requires, He sees it for what it is—an act of willful pride. And as Peter reminds us, He resists the proud! (1 Peter 5:5). That sounds like a clear clue as to why some of us feel kept at arm's length from Jesus.

Letting God's people go was a tough task for Pharaoh. The Israelites comprised the heart of Egypt's labor force. They were the backbone of the economy. God had asked the Egyptian king to do something of great difficulty and phenomenal risk. When he refused, Moses said to him, "Why do you refuse to humble yourself before God?"

Jesus humbled Himself and became obedient unto death, even the death of the cross (Philippians 2:8). Which is exactly Paul's point about meeting Jesus by becoming conformed to His death (Philippians 3:10).

THE THIRD MEETING PLACE...
Total Surrender

Paul writes that the third way to experience Jesus in our lives is by a willing conformity to His death (3:10). Again, we cannot think of this in terms of the Crucifixion alone. This is not about dying so that we can get to heaven to experience Jesus there. It's about coming to grips with the dynamics of Jesus' death and conforming our lives to that pattern.

Actually, the death of Jesus began long before the Cross, in eternity past when Jesus willingly surrendered to the Father's decree that He should die for the sins of the world. In our history, that surrender was reenacted in the garden of Gethsemane. There, while His friends slept, He went through the excruciating pain of the heaviest decision of His life. His Father was asking Him to go to the cross, where the pain and torment of the sins of the world would press upon His sinless soul while soldiers mocked and curious bystanders gawked.

The Gospels record that the grief of this decision was so wrenching He literally sweated drops of blood in the process. Every sweat gland is surrounded by a whole network of tiny blood vessels; this is how our body cools itself. The moment of extreme crisis was so intense for Jesus that these vessels burst under the pressure. This decision wracked every aspect of His being. The cost was beyond measure, beyond comprehension.

It is not surprising, then, that Jesus in His humanity shrank from the horror—asking His Father if there might not be another way. But in the end, through lips parched with anxiety, in a voice heavy with the weight of the cross to come, He uttered those unforgettable words of unparalleled resolve, "Not My will, but Yours be done!"

Being conformed to His death means *full surrender* to our Father's will—regardless. No excuses. No escape clauses. No negotiation. And not only is it surrender for the moment, it is about *persevering* in the resolve until we have fully obeyed. As an exhausted Jesus rose from His prayer, He could see the torches of the approaching lynch mob. Judas stepped forward and betrayed the Lord of life with a kiss of death. Jesus could have lashed out at Judas, blamed the whole mess on him, told the authorities that they were in league with a man whose motives were highly suspect.

But Jesus would not be deterred. When Peter unsheathed his sword and slashed one of the servants across the face, severing the man's ear, Jesus had every right to escalate the conflict. He could have called twelve legions of angels, exercising His rights and power in the perfectly justifiable defense of innocence. Instead, He persevered in surrender. Foreshadowing what He was about to do at the cross, He loved His enemies and healed the wounded man's ear.

It's one thing to surrender. It's quite another to perse-
vere when we're presented with opportunities to justifiably
slide out of our resolve. Through all of those horrible hours
to follow, when the faultlessly righteous Jesus was dragged
through the halls of the kangaroo courts, He refused to
return their accusations and slander.

Peter was there. He knew. Years later he would pen,
"Christ also suffered for you, leaving you an example for you
to follow in His steps…while being reviled, He did not revile
in return; while suffering, He uttered no threats, but kept
entrusting Himself to Him who judges righteously" (1 Peter
2:21, 23).

This is the pattern we are to follow in our lives if we are
to know Jesus. An undaunted and nonnegotiable loyalty to
Jesus—regardless of the cost—is the key to a deepening,
intimate fellowship with Him. Regardless of what He
requires, those who want to draw close to Him meet Him at
that sweat-stained rock in the Garden and brokenly repeat
His words after Him: "Not my will, but Yours be done."

It is a resolve that covers the whole waterfront of our
existence. Nothing is exempt. Relationships, real estate,
financial resources, spouses, children, grandchildren,
desires, dreams, plans, attitudes, and actions are all
included.

It calls for the bold and determined cessation of that
fulfilling affair.

It demands no flirting around the edges of sensuality and the immediate resolve to eliminate opportunities for voyeuristic pleasure with pornography.

It requires the expulsion of jealousy, residual anger, and the bitterness that tear at our relationships. Gethsemane asks for it all. Stay at the rock until there is nothing held back. Then rise, take up your cross, and follow Him. Remember, no cross is heavier than His was. When we are committed to rejoicing in the Lord rather than ourselves and value Jesus and His perfect will more than our own rights, privileges, and possessions, the cross of surrender will be an honor, not a burden.

But there is more. Think with me for a minute. We know that the theme of the Cross is love. Love, in fact, for those who have deeply offended God in their sin and rebellion. And Jesus was giving His very lifeblood for these people.

He was dying for the Pharisees…who falsely accused.

He was dying for the soldiers…who were caustically cruel.

He was dying for the Sanhedrin…who broke their own laws to condemn Him.

He was dying for Pilate…who caved in to political pressure.

He was dying for Herod…who mocked and sneered.

He was dying for His executioners…who had no mercy.

He was dying for all those who throughout history past and ages to come would mock and spit in the face of His Father whom He loved.

And He was dying for me and you, while we were still in our sin and rebellion.

Simply put, the heart of the Cross is about loving our enemies. It is about mercy for those who deserved nothing but retribution. It is about taking the rap for someone else, about doing justice for the unjust. Being "conformed to His death" means that I am willing to forgive those who have cruelly offended me, commit acts of love toward those who deserve my scorn, and take the rap for my enemies when necessary. I do these things understanding that God Himself will ultimately deal with my offenders in a just and righteous way. But more importantly, I conform because this is where I meet Jesus.

BOB'S COSTLY DECISION

Why did Bob meet with such frustration and disappointment when he sought to draw near to Jesus? The answer goes way back to his boyhood days. Bob's dad had left his mother when he was young. But not so young that he didn't live with the awful memories of the cruel abuse. Bob's dad had multiple affairs with women all over town, and he finally ran off with and married his wife's best friend. He lives in a town not far from Bob, and Bob long ago vowed that he would never forgive his dad.

The risk was too great.

The fear of further rejection too strong.

The thought of dredging up old pain too daunting.

The prospect of restoring that broken relationship too great a mountain to climb.

So Bob didn't make contact. He refused to move one inch toward reconciliation. In his mind, this was the last person on earth to merit his love and forgiveness. In this area of Bob's life, so near to the center of his heart, he refused to be conformed to the image of Christ's death. He refused to kneel with Jesus in Gethsemane and face the excruciating prospect of encountering and forgiving his dad. The words *not my will but Yours be done* had not crossed Bob's lips, let alone his heart.

Jesus cannot draw near to a heart steeled against His will. Experiencing Him in the fullness of His presence requires that we go with Him to the Garden and kneel in surrender, conforming to what He did—for even the most undeserving in our lives. In that light, full surrender—*regardless of the cost*—is always sweet surrender. For it is within such surrender that we come to know and experience Jesus in deeper and fuller ways.

And so He waits for us. Waits for us to love and value Him more than ourselves…waits to meet us. And when we meet Him, the experience of His presence delights our soul and makes us long for more.

THE PRAYER OF
THE SEEKER

Those who experience the pleasure of His presence have made their lives *simply about Jesus.*

They live to meet Him wherever He is found: in the wilderness of Satan's attack…in the suffering that He bore because He loved us…and at that rock in Gethsemane where surrender claimed its finest hour.

Dear Lord, from the depths of my heart I ask for complete cleansing. Grant me the grace to keep self in its proper place, and to make my life simply about You. In the midst of all my routines, successes, and disappointments, help me to always rejoice in You and value You above any earthly prize. Meet me in temptation, and deliver me from evil. And if I should suffer, help me to pause to feel Your pain and love You more for the way You suffered for me. Jesus, I will live this day on bended knee by Your side in Gethsemane. What You ask I will do.

Thank You for the promise that You will reward those who diligently seek You. I do seek You—with all my heart. I humbly ask that in Your good time and in Your way, You would satisfy my heart with the experience of Your presence.

In Your worthy name I pray. Amen.

*Behold, I stand at the door and knock;
if anyone hears My voice
and opens the door,
I will come in to him
and will dine with him,
and he with Me.
—Jesus Christ, Lord of the universe*

REVELATION 3:20

Simply Jesus.

The message is quite simple, isn't it?

We need no more and no less.

Evangelist D.L. Moody once said, "When God gave Christ to this world, He gave the best He had, and He wants us to do the same … Make up your mind that your life is going to be given to that one thing."

What is that "one thing" for you? Are you going to dedicate yourself to Jesus? Simply Jesus? No more and no less?

It's our pleasure to be a part of your faith journey. As you continue to grow, our prayer is that you would trust in Christ and commit yourself to Him in all that you do and say. And may you *experience the One your heart longs for!*

Live for Him,
The 24-7 Ministries Team

The Heart of a Tender Warrior
Becoming a Man of Purpose
Stu Weber ISBN 1-59052-039-4

Be what every woman dreams of, what every boy desires to be, and what every man yearns most to become. Bestselling author and pastor Stu Weber shows you how to be a tender warrior.

The Power of Crying Out
When Prayer Becomes Mighty
Bill Gothard ISBN 1-59052-037-8

Bill Gothard explains how a crisis that is humanly impossible is an opportunity for God to show His power—the moment you cry out to Him.

God Is Up to Something Great
Turning Your Yesterdays into Better Tomorrows
Tony Evans ISBN 1-59052-038-6

Are you living with regrets? Discover the positives of your past. Tony Evans shows how God intends to use your experiences—good, bad, and ugly—to lead you toward His purpose for your life.

Six Steps to Spiritual Revival
God's Awesome Power in Your Life
Pat Robertson ISBN 1-59052-055-6

Pat Robertson reveals an amazing Scriptural pattern of transformation when people hunger for God's presence. Experience personal revival—let the unique qualities God has placed within you bear fruit for His glory!

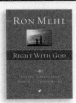

LIFECHANGE BOOKS

IN THE SECRET PLACE
For God and You Alone
J. OTIS LEDBETTER ISBN 1-59052-252-4

Receive answers to some of life's most perplexing questions—and find deeper fellowship alone in the place where God dwells.

OUR JEALOUS GOD
Love That Won't Let Me Go
BILL GOTHARD ISBN 1-59052-225-7

God's intense jealousy for you is your highest honor, an overflowing of sheer grace. And when you understand it better, it becomes a pathway to countless blessings.

A LITTLE POT OF OIL
JILL BRISCOE ISBN 1-59052-234-6

What if He's asking you to pour out more than you can give? Step into the forward motion of God's love—and find the power of the Holy Spirit!

HOW GOOD IS GOOD ENOUGH?
ANDY STANLEY ISBN 1-59052-274-5

Find out why Jesus taught that goodness is not even a requirement to enter heaven—and why Christianity is beyond fair.

www.bigchangemoments.com